NATIONAL AUDIT OFFICE

REPORT BY THE
COMPTROLLER AND
AUDITOR GENERAL

Ministry of Defence: British Army in Germany—Drawdown of Equipment and Stores

ORDERED BY
THE HOUSE OF COMMONS
TO BE PRINTED
13 APRIL 1994

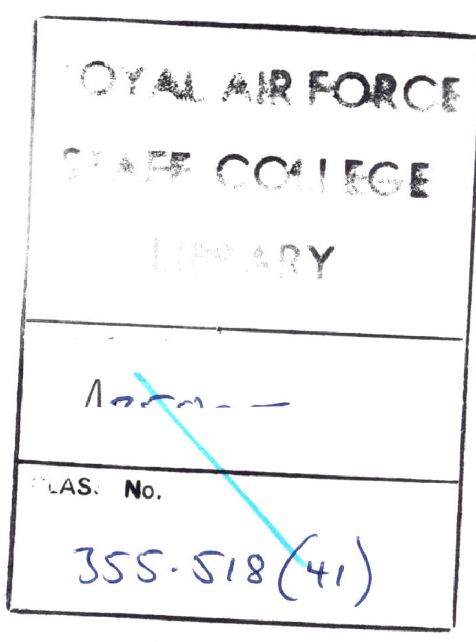

LONDON: HMSO
344

£6.70 NET

This report has been prepared under Section 6 of the National Audit Act 1983 for presentation to the House of Commons in accordance with Section 9 of the Act.

John Bourn
Comptroller and Auditor General

National Audit Office
8 April 1994

The Comptroller and Auditor General is the head of the National Audit Office employing some 800 staff. He, and the NAO, are totally independent of Government. He certifies the accounts of all Government departments and a wide range of other public sector bodies; and he has statutory authority to report to Parliament on the economy, efficiency and effectiveness with which departments and other bodies have used their resources.

Contents

Summary and conclusions

1 In July 1990, The Government's Options for Change review announced a fundamental restructuring of Britain's Armed Forces. Reductions in the size of the British Army of the Rhine are a major part of that process. These started in 1991 with the Early Closures Programme. This was followed in 1992 by the start of the main Drawdown, which is being phased over three years up to April 1995. Drawdown is taking place during a period of unparalleled change in the Ministry of Defence (the Department), and is by far the largest move of troops and equipment undertaken by the British Army in modern times.

2 The National Audit Office examined how drawdown of equipment and stores was progressing and whether the Department were maximising the financial benefits. The Department responded positively to the emerging findings of the study by taking action where appropriate.

On the planning and progress of Drawdown

3 The main Drawdown Programme, which was influenced by the Department's desire to return premises no longer required to the German Government as quickly as possible, was well planned with clear milestones to enable progress to be monitored. The programme was sufficiently flexible to cope with changing circumstances, with timely and detailed guidance given to units. The Early Closures Programme, however, which was aimed at generating early savings, was planned with insufficient regard to the logistics requirements of Drawdown. Savings from Early Closures in the period to April 1995 are estimated by the Department to be £35 million a year which, though £24 million a year less than previously predicted, are still substantial. Drawdown has been underway at a time of unparalleled upheaval and conflicting pressures, notably from Operation Granby and operations in the former Yugoslavia. Nevertheless, by the end of Phase 1 in March 1993, the Department had achieved the unit moves and closures aimed for in that phase, and had drawn down large quantities of a wide range of equipment and stores (paragraphs 2.2–2.20).

4 Unit moves and closures in Germany are part of the Army's ongoing transition to its new role in support of the Allied Command Europe Rapid Reaction Corps. The Department have undertaken a major rationalisation of equipment support and base repair activities to make them more responsive to the needs of a smaller, more mobile, Army (paragraphs 2.21–2.23). It is important, however, that the Department:

(a) review the future of the stores depot at Dulmen in Germany as planned, and guard against excessive stockholdings by completing their review of units' equipment and stores entitlements in the light of new requirements. The major part of this work has now been completed (paragraphs 2.24–2.26);

(b)   continue with their plan to extend their visibility of stocks held at units in Germany. This should allow greater control and flexibility in the management and procurement of stocks (paragraphs 2.27–2.28); and

(c)   review the scope for adjusting reprovisioning as soon as future support policy is finalised. The Department have already taken advantage of Drawdown and reductions in the size of the Army to reduce their provisioning spend on stores by about 20 per cent over 1991–92 and 1992–93 (paragraphs 2.29–2.32).

On the Drawdown of equipment and stores

5 Vehicles form a large proportion by volume and value of the equipment being drawn down, and many have already been returned to the United Kingdom. However, there was a build-up of vehicles awaiting processing at the overspill storage site for vehicles returned to the United Kingdom. In December 1992 the Theatre Drawdown Unit in Germany held about 1,600 vehicles pending decisions about what was to be done with them — their original purchase price was some £74 million, although some of the older vehicles had little residual value. By March 1993 the number had increased to approximately 1,800 of which 1,100 were unserviceable. Most were stored in the open. Around 35 per cent of the vehicles, including some from the old Reserve stock, had been on the site for over 12 months (paragraphs 3.2–3.10).

6 As the Department have yet to complete their review of manpower and equipment needs for the post-Options for Change Army, they are unable to determine their precise global requirements for vehicles. The effect has been to delay decisions on whether to keep vehicles in Germany, return them to the United Kingdom or sell them. Nevertheless, by February 1994 the number of vehicles at the Theatre Drawdown Unit had decreased to 716 (paragraphs 3.6–3.10).

7 As regards the large volume of technical and general stores being drawndown, the National Audit Office identified the following areas which merit the Department's continuing attention:

(a)   the need to avoid additional handling costs incurred in sending items to the Theatre Drawdown Unit and subsequently redirecting them to the disposals unit (paragraph 3.14);

(b)   the costs and benefits of returning low value items to store. Although the total value of such stores recovered amounted to £2.25 million, the average value of 76 per cent of items returned was £7 (paragraph 3.15);

(c)   the liaison arrangements between Germany and supply depots in the United Kingdom. Issues of stores had been made to the previous address of 26 units which had moved. The Department have now taken steps which should ensure that the problem does not recur (paragraph 3.18);

(d)   the need to avoid recurrence of significant delays in processing items returned to store. At one stage some 120 containers had been awaiting attention for 12 months or more because containers returned from the Gulf conflict had to be cleared first. Delays in processing meant that the Department were unable to take account of returned items when reprovisioning, but they expect similar problems to be avoided in the future by the introduction of new computer systems (paragraph 3.19); and

(e)   the need to complete their review of base repair equipments stored at Dulmen to determine their future location (paragraph 3.21).

8 Drawdown is an opportunity to generate income by selling surplus items. In 1992–93 receipts from sales in Germany amounted to £5.18 million, mostly in respect of vehicles, and the Department expect further receipts of £8.5 million by April 1995 (paragraphs 3.23–3.25). In seeking maximum benefit from Drawdown, the Department should:

(a)   do more to ensure that where possible vehicles are sold in Germany rather than, as has sometimes been the case, in the United Kingdom. This saves transportation costs and prices in Germany are generally higher. In this regard, the Department are now taking steps to ensure closer co-ordination between Germany and the United Kingdom in deciding which vehicles should be returned to the United Kingdom (paragraph 3.25);

(b)   cannibalise sales vehicles only when it is essential and cost effective, and continue to explore the possibility of enhancing the sales value of vehicles by making minor repairs to turn them into "runners" (paragraph 3.25); and

(c)   ensure that vehicle requirements across the three Services have been met before disposing of surpluses (paragraph 3.26).

On the movement and control of equipment and stores

9 The marginal costs of using Service transport and drivers are less than the full cost of the commercial option and, where possible, the Department use military vehicles and personnel. However, the Department do use commercial carriers, and in the cases examined they used competitive tendering to obtain best value (paragraphs 4.2–4.4).

10 In October 1992 the Department had to hire a commercial roll-on roll-off vessel, the NORNEWS SERVICE, to replace their own vessel which had been diverted to operations in the former Yugoslavia. The ferry was used primarily to resupply British Forces in Germany, but also assisted in the Drawdown Programme. The Department selected the NORNEWS SERVICE, as the cheapest vessel of five which met the specification, from a tender list of ten ships. However, there was not a full record of the tender analysis in that the comparative capability of the ten ships was not recorded. In the seven month period reviewed by the National Audit Office the full capacity of the vessel was not used.

Nevertheless, the Department stated that they were still able to move more equipment than would have been possible using their own vessel (paragraphs 4.5–4.8).

11 Maintaining normal standards of accounting and control during a period of exceptional upheaval is not easy, but in general units drawing down have achieved this. Once units close, responsibility for clearing their store accounts is transferred to other, "custodial", units. But clearance is going to be a major task. By February 1994 only four of the accounts of the 116 units which had closed or moved had been cleared. These included the accounts for two of the seven units which had been closed for more than 23 months. The volume of transactions to be cleared on any one account can be considerable, and many more units have yet to close (paragraphs 4.9–4.13). To strengthen their controls, the Department need:

(a)   a clear plan to contain and reduce the backlog of uncleared accounts, and to ensure that discrepancies are properly investigated. They should aim to resolve the accounting problems and equipment discrepancies at the very large 23 Base Workshop in Germany before the unit account is passed on to custodial units (paragraphs 4.12–4.15 and 4.19);

(b)   to give particular attention to uncleared transactions and accounting discrepancies relating to valuable and attractive items. Having identified cases relating to firearms, the National Audit Office notified the Department who responded quickly and undertook an investigation. They confirmed that no physical loss had occurred and that all weapons had been accounted for. They are investigating a discrepancy relating to a voucher for plastic explosives and have advised that the results of initial investigations suggested that the explosive and associated items had been properly consumed during training and that further work was in hand to confirm this (paragraphs 4.13–4.17);

(c)   to ensure that vouchers acknowledging receipt of items are not returned to closed units and to be alive to difficulties which may arise when custodial units close and accounting responsibility is again transferred (paragraphs 4.14–4.15); and

(d)   to remind units of the need to maintain normal stocktaking throughout their drawdown period unless prior approval is given by the appropriate stores accounting/stocktaking authority (paragraph 4.19).

Overall conclusions

12 Drawdown of equipment and stores is driven by unit moves and closures, which in Phase 1 progressed broadly according to plan. The availability of accommodation and storage facilities for the even larger numbers of moves and closures scheduled for Phases 2 and 3 will continue to present problems. The Department are aware of this and of the need to make a concerted effort if they are to complete Drawdown by March 1995.

13 The study findings should be seen in the context of the highly demanding logistical challenge which the scale and timing of Drawdown present. However, this Report identifies a number of matters, many of which the Department have now taken into account in their continuing efforts to ensure that the drawdown of equipment and stores progresses smoothly, and that maximum benefit is obtained. Indeed the National Audit Office study was undertaken at an early stage in the drawdown process specifically for that purpose.

14 Naturally, the Department's focus has been on the physical task of handling the vast quantities of items being drawn down. They recognise, however, the importance of maintaining effective accounting and control, and are conscious of the need for this aspect to be given particular attention as Drawdown proceeds.

Part 1: Introduction

1.1 In July 1990, the Government's Options for Change review announced a fundamental re-structuring of Britain's Armed Forces in the light of changing international circumstances. The objective was for smaller, better equipped forces, that were properly trained and housed, and well motivated. Reduction in the size of the British Army of the Rhine was to be a major part of that process.

1.2 Action by the Ministry of Defence (the Department) to reduce the Army in Germany started in 1991 with their Early Closures Programme, an initiative designed to achieve an early peace dividend. This was followed in April 1992 by the start of their main "Drawdown" programme. Drawdown is being implemented in three twelve-month phases over the three years to April 1995. The programme involves the redeployment of units within Germany, their repatriation to the United Kingdom or their disbandment. It is by far the largest move of troops and equipment undertaken by the British Army in modern times.

1.3 Before 1991 there were approximately 50 main Army locations in Germany. These included schools, hospitals, barracks and headquarters, together with essential logistic support organisations such as workshops and stores depots. The value of stores held was about £1.3 billion. Drawdown will involve the closure of installations at some 30 locations and the re-deployment of equipment and stores within Germany, their return to stock in Germany or the United Kingdom, or their disposal through the Department's Defence Sales Organisation.

1.4 The Department expect that by 1995, the British Army in Germany will have 27,000 fewer Service personnel, a reduction of over 50 per cent; 11,000 fewer locally employed civilians; 2,900 fewer armoured vehicles such as tanks and armoured personnel carriers, and 18,000 fewer non-armoured vehicles. It will reduce from three armoured divisions to one. By the end of Drawdown, some 72,000 Service and civilian personnel and their dependents will have returned to the United Kingdom.

1.5 Drawdown is taking place during a period of unparalleled upheaval, uncertainty and change in the Department. In addition to their participation in Operation Granby and in support of United Nations operations in the former Republic of Yugoslavia, the Department have been involved in the introduction of a New Management Strategy, unit amalgamations and disbandments, the restructuring of the logistic corps of the Army and a fundamental reorganisation of the Army's logistic support.

Scope of the National Audit Office examination

1.6 Mindful of the considerable equipment and stores holdings in Germany and the significant changes in force levels and geographic locations resulting from the Army's Drawdown Programme, the National Audit Office examined how Drawdown of equipment and stores was proceeding and whether the Department were maximising the financial benefits. The results are set out in the following parts of this report:

Part 2: Planning, and overall progress, of Drawdown;

Part 3: the Drawdown of Equipment and Stores;

Part 4: the Movement and Control of Equipment and Stores.

1.7 In carrying out their study the National Audit Office visited Headquarters and units in Germany and the United Kingdom. Much of their work was undertaken during an early stage of Drawdown so that the Department could take the results into account. To this end, the Department were given regular feedback on the emerging findings as the study progressed. They responded positively by taking action where appropriate.

Part 2: Planning, and overall progress, of Drawdown

2.1 The National Audit Office study focused on the equipment and stores implications of Drawdown, but in the wider context of unit moves and closures since the two are inextricably linked. Such moves and closures determine the timing, type and quantity of equipment and stores drawn down. And, as they reflect the changing role of the Army in Germany, they also shape the Department's equipment and stores requirements. Part 2 therefore examines the Department's planning for drawdown; the progress they have made in withdrawing units from Germany, and in drawing down equipment and stores; and what the Department have done to shape equipment and stores support in Germany to match operational commitments.

How well Drawdown has been planned

Audit criteria

Whether the Department have set time and financial criteria to permit monitoring of Drawdown.

Whether there is guidance to units on managing Drawdown economically, efficiently and to the required timescale.

2.2 The Department developed detailed plans for the amalgamation and disbandment of units, and for unit moves within Germany and elsewhere. These plans set out milestones, which have provided a clear basis for the Department's monitoring of progress. At the same time, the plans have proved sufficiently flexible to allow the Department to adapt to changing circumstances. The National Audit Office did not examine the Department's priorities for unit moves and closures, which reflected military judgements and the desire to return premises no longer required to the German Government as quickly as possible. Nevertheless, in formulating their plan, the Department took into consideration such factors as: operational requirements; training facilities; maintenance costs; and the quality of life. The Department's Internal Audit found that the basic ingredients of a financial appraisal had been employed, but were concerned that subsequent changes to the plan were not always accompanied by a full cost statement of the implications. The Department confirmed that full financial appraisals are now conducted as a matter of routine when changes to the plan are to be considered.

2.3 Although the Department have budgetary control systems for their day-to-day management of the British Army of the Rhine, they did not set separate financial criteria by which to monitor Drawdown. They told the National Audit Office it would have been impracticable and costly to put in place the systems necessary to identify costs relating to Drawdown generally, and for equipment and stores in particular. Moreover, the introduction and operation of special to purpose systems could not be achieved in the timescale necessary to capture much of the data.

2.4 The Department's broad plans for unit moves and closures have been complemented by detailed guidance and advice to individual units. They set out for units a "critical path" of key events designed to enable units to conduct drawdown in a timely, economic and efficient manner. Specialist teams have visited every unit drawing down at an early stage to identify items of equipment likely to be required and those that could be sent for disposal. The Department's written guidance to units has been constantly refined and is generally comprehensive. It was regarded by the units visited by the National Audit Office as a valuable planning aid.

2.5 As a general rule, units have about a year in which to complete drawdown. Provided key milestones are met it is for each unit to manage its own plan in the light of its particular operational and training commitments.

Audit Criterion

Whether the Drawdown programme follows an order conducive to economic and efficient processing of equipment and stores.

2.6 Drawdown was preceded in 1991 by the Early Closure Programme which was planned and executed to a tight schedule, and in advance of the detailed planning undertaken for Drawdown.

2.7 The conventional pattern of large scale movements is that the logistic infrastructure remains in place until the forward units have drawn down through it. However, under the Early Closure Programme, seven logistic and support units were closed. This resulted in a reduction of 2,800 civilian, and 600 military, posts and the loss of a large proportion of the Department's logistic base in Germany. This has had a considerable impact on the implementation of the later stages of Drawdown:

(a) the vehicle depots at Antwerp and Recklinghausen and the Ordnance Services Unit at Viersen in Germany, which had a responsibility for processing stores returned from units, were disbanded under the Early Closure Programme. A Theatre Drawdown Unit was therefore established at Moenchengladbach in early 1992 to assume a "clearing house" role for equipments, stores and non-armoured vehicles being drawndown. It also subsumed some of the other responsibilities previously discharged at Viersen and elsewhere, such as issuing maintenance stocks and holding specialist vehicles. This organisation employs 150 military and civilian staff and has an annual manpower cost of £2.5 million, although not all staff costs are Drawdown related. The Department have had difficulty in recruiting good calibre civilian staff for the Theatre Drawdown Unit on what would be a short term commitment; and

(b) the closure of 37 Rhine Workshop and other smaller workshops during Early Closures created problems for the logistic services generally in providing

engineering support to maintain vehicles stored at the Theatre Drawdown Unit (paragraph 3.8), and in dealing with vehicles and equipments returned unserviceable from the Gulf conflict.

2.8 In 1990 the Department predicted savings of £59 million a year from March 1992 onwards as a direct result of the early Closure Programme, and the exercise has provided lessons which they were able to apply when implementing the main Drawdown. However, because of the need to establish the Theatre Drawdown Unit and relocate other services and activities removed in the Early Closures Programme, the Department's estimate is now that the annual savings from Early Closures during the three year period of Drawdown will amount to £35 million. This figure excludes redundancy payments and other costs, such as those associated with additional contract vehicle repair, which are not readily quantifiable.

Main points:

2.9 **The main Drawdown Programme was well planned, with clear milestones and valuable guidance to units. The Early Closures Programme, however, had insufficient regard to the logistics requirements of the later stages of Drawdown. Savings, though still substantial, have been lower than expected.**

How well Drawdown is progressing

Audit Criterion

Whether Drawdown is progressing to the Department's required timescale.

2.10 In addition to the Early Closures Programme, other factors have affected the Department's ability to manage Drawdown smoothly. The recovery to Germany of equipment and stores after the Gulf conflict caused particular difficulty occurring, as it did, during the Early Closures Programme and at the start of Phase 1. However, the problem was eased by the fact that some equipment sent to the Gulf from Germany was returned directly to the United Kingdom. More recently, increased commitments in Northern Ireland and operations in the former Yugoslavia have necessarily diverted logistic resources from Drawdown, and forced changes to the order in which specific units drawdown.

2.11 During Early Closures and Phase 1 of Drawdown the Department had considerable difficulty providing timely and suitable accommodation in the United Kingdom for some repatriated units and their equipments. They also had difficulty establishing suitable storage facilities for equipments and stores surplus to the needs of units remaining in Germany, but for which there remained a continued Service requirement (paragraphs 3.10 and 3.21). These difficulties, which were compounded by the influx of material returning from the Gulf, were a factor in the Department's decision to establish the Theatre Drawdown Unit in Germany to act as a filter for equipment and stores being drawn down.

2.12 Three out of 23 units which returned to the United Kingdom were placed in temporary accommodation whilst building or renovation took place at their intended base. Others moved direct to their future long-term location with rebuilds or works improvement being undertaken whilst they were in residence. Transitional funding for works services in the order of £400 million has been earmarked for use in the three years of the Drawdown Programme to establish accommodation suited to the operational and domestic needs of repatriated units.

2.13 Unit moves and closures have not, therefore, progressed as smoothly as the Department originally planned. The Department have, of necessity, made adjustments to their plan in terms of which units were to move, and when. Nevertheless, at the end of Phase 1 in March 1993 they had moved or closed 59 headquarters, major units and depots, and 50 minor units; the same number as originally planned in August 1991. A total of 164 units are scheduled to be disbanded or moved in Phases 2 and 3 of Drawdown.

Overall progress in drawing down equipment and stores

2.14 Some units involved in Drawdown simply withdraw from Germany and relocate in their present form, taking most of their equipment and stores with them. However, as other units move, amalgamate or close a vast range of material is being redeployed, returned to stock or sold — anything ranging from pickaxe handles to major tank assemblies. Equipment and stores are regarded as drawn down when a unit releases those items surplus to its future requirements.

2.15 To give a measure of the scale of drawdown, Figure 1 shows the volume of vehicles, ammunition, technical, general and accommodation stores drawn down by 31 March 1993. It also includes the Department's estimates for Phases 2 and 3. The figures represent items returned to stock or sent for disposal. They exclude those which have been redeployed between units.

2.16 The Department did not set separate milestones by which to monitor progress in drawing down equipment and stores, because the timing depends entirely on progress with unit moves and closures. However, as Figure 1 shows, they have already drawn down large quantities of a wide range of material. By the end of Phase 1 this included nearly three-quarters of the armoured vehicles they expect to drawdown by 1995; almost half of the non-armoured vehicles; over a third of the technical and general stores and half the ammunition.

2.17 Of the 10,000 tons of ammunition drawn down, 2,000 were destroyed. A further 10,000 tons of mainly 105 mm ammunition, valued at £10,000 a ton, is due to be returned to the United Kingdom during the remainder of Drawdown. This will leave a surplus of certain types of ammunition in Germany which, rather than return to the United Kingdom with resulting transportation costs, will be retained there and expended in training over the next three to five years.

2.18 By the end of Phase 1 over 4,000 cubic metres of accommodation stores had been returned to the United Kingdom, and 10,000 cubic metres sent for disposal by sale in Germany. But this represents a little over a quarter of the volume that the Department expect to repatriate or send for disposal by the end of April 1995.

Figure 1: Situation Report as at end of Phase 1 of Drawdown

Phase 1: Armoured Vehicles drawn down	1,950
Phases 2&3: projected drawdown quantities	950
Phase 1: B Vehicles drawn down	7,200
Phases 2&3: projected drawdown quantities	8,000+
Phase 1: Motor Transport, Technical and General Stores drawn down	662,000 items
Phases 2&3: projected drawdown quantities	1,000,000+ items
Phase 1: Ammunition drawn down	10,000 tons
Phases 2&3: projected drawdown quantities	10,000 tons
Phase 1: Accommodation Stores drawn down	$14,000m^3$
Phases 2&3: projected drawdown quantities	$40,000m^3$

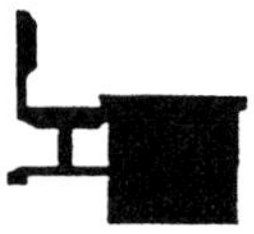

Source: Ministry of Defence

Figure 1 shows the volume of vehicles, general stores, ammunition and accommodation stores drawn down by 31 March 1993, and the Department's estimates for Phases 2 and 3.

Main points:

2.19 **Unit moves and closures have taken place during a difficult period, and there have been accommodation constraints in the United Kingdom. Nevertheless, at the end of Phase I of Drawdown the Department had achieved their objectives — despite conflicting pressures from operational commitments.**

2.20 **The Department have already drawn down large quantities of a wide range of items. However, with almost three quarters of accommodation stores and half the ammunition still to be drawn down, the Department should continue to monitor the process to ensure they remain on schedule.**

Shaping equipment and stores support in Germany to match operational commitments

2.21 Unit moves and closures in Germany are part of the Army's ongoing transition to their new role in support of the Allied Command Europe Rapid Reaction Corps which will differ significantly from that of the former British Army of the Rhine. The National Audit Office therefore sought to establish what the Department had done to ensure that equipment and stores support in Germany is tailored to this new role.

Audit Criteria

Whether equipment and stores support has been adjusted to reflect the British Army of the Rhine's changing operational role.

Whether the Department have sufficient management information to help ensure that equipment and stores holdings are the minimum required.

2.22 The Department have undertaken major reviews and rationalisation of equipment support and base repair activities to make them more responsive to the needs of a smaller, more mobile, Army. With the closure of the last remaining base workshop in Germany during Phase 2 of Drawdown, major overhauls of equipment will, in future, be concentrated solely in the United Kingdom.

2.23 The Army have a "One Base Concept" for the control and issue of mechanical transport, technical and general stores. A major principle behind the Concept was that stockholdings would be visible to the Centre, providing a more economic management of the inventory. Stock held at Dulmen in Germany would form part of the central inventory and demands would be satisfied from either Dulmen, or from depots in the United Kingdom.

2.24 At the outset of Drawdown the Department's intention was that stocks at Dulmen would be issued in preference to stocks from the United Kingdom, and that Dulmen would be restocked only by returns resulting from

Drawdown. Eventually, therefore, stocks at Dulmen would have been exhausted. In the latter half of 1992, the Department decided that stocks held at Dulmen would be primarily for use in Germany and were to be used to satisfy demands from other theatres only where these cannot be met by United Kingdom depots. The Department are now considering the long-term viability of Dulmen, particularly in relation to their study into the establishment of the Army Base Supply and Distribution Agency.

2.25 In 1992, the Department's Internal Audit highlighted the problems of delayed decisions on future equipment entitlements and stock holding policies in Germany. They considered that such delays created the danger of over-retention in both the United Kingdom and Germany, and of increased storage and transportation costs of items which could well be surplus to requirements.

2.26 The Department recognise the problem, and the task of tailoring the equipment and stores holdings of individual units in Germany to reflect their changing role is underway. The major part of this work, the determination of the global equipment liabilities, has now been completed and the individual unit equipment and stores entitlement review which follows is a continuing process. At the time of the National Audit Office examination they had finalised their assessment of the equipment and stores entitlements of some 60 per cent of units.

Stockholdings and provisioning

2.27 Central to the Department's "One Base Concept" (paragraph 2.23) and overall aim of rationalising global stock holdings, is their policy of gaining increased knowledge (or "visibility") and, therefore, control of stocks held. By this means they should be in a better position to ensure that future procurement decisions are based on total, rather than partial, holdings. Before 1991, the Army in Germany had visibility of equipment and stores held in their main storage depot at Dulmen, visibility of holdings in some secondary depots but none of stocks held at unit level.

2.28 The closure of the Inventory Control Point at Viersen during the Early Closure Programme transferred visibility and control to the United Kingdom of the £120 million of stock held at Dulmen. By the end of 1993, the Department had extended their visibility and control to all secondary depots in Germany where they estimate that in excess of £50 million of stock is held. Eventually, they aim to have central sight of holdings in Germany down to unit level, which the Department estimate have a value of some £70 million. The Department expect to achieve this enhanced visibility, and greater flexibility in their total management of stocks, by mid 1996 through the introduction of computer systems under Project UNICOM.

2.29 Because many factors influence global stock levels, including substantial returns from the Gulf conflict, the National Audit Office were unable to identify precisely what the effect of drawdown of equipment and stores on stock levels had been. Nevertheless, there have been significant increases of some items from the levels that existed before the build-up for the Gulf conflict. For instance, the value of general stores holdings has increased by some £9 million, whilst the value of those for motor transport and technical stores has increased by £209 million (57 per cent) and £82 million (41 per cent) respectively.

2.30 In the light of these increases, coupled with the advent of a smaller Army, the National Audit Office sought to establish what effect there had been on reprovisioning purchases. The Department explained, however, that for the most part there was not a direct link between drawdown and provisioning. On the one hand, equipment drawn down was being used to make good historical shortfalls. On the other hand it was often being replaced by more modern and technologically advanced, and therefore more expensive, equipment.

2.31 The Department acknowledged that as this was a rapidly changing area with a number of decisions still to be taken on future support policy, the full potential for reducing forward provisioning as a result of returned stores was not yet clear. However, they had reduced their provisioning spend on stores by about 20 per cent (approximately £42 million) across the board over the period 1991–92 and 1992–93 to compensate for Drawdown returns and reductions in the size of the Army. And they gave two specific examples where savings had been made which they attributed to Drawdown:

- the accommodation stores budget was cut by £10 million in 1992–93 in anticipation of surpluses being used to offset much of what would otherwise have been purchased to meet global requirements; and

- components from some equipments scheduled for destruction under the Conventional Forces Europe Treaty arrangements were being salvaged within the Treaty regulations. The Department estimated that this had saved £5 million worth of armoured vehicle assemblies.

Main Points:

2.32 **The Department are taking steps to ensure that equipment and stores support reflect the changing role of the Army in Germany:**

- **they are soon to transfer major overhaul work to the United Kingdom;**

- **to guard against excessive stockholdings, they are reviewing the equipment and stores entitlements of individual units as part of a continuing process;**

- **they are continuing with their plan to extend visibility of stock holdings in Germany down to unit level;**

- **they are reviewing the future of the stores depot at Dulmen, taking account of the significantly reduced force levels in Germany and their extensive depot capacity in the United Kingdom; and**

- **they plan to review the scope for adjusting reprovisioning as soon as the position on future support policy is finalised.**

Part 3: The Drawdown of equipment and stores

3.1 Part 3 sets out the National Audit Office's observations on practical aspects of drawing down equipment and stores, including disposals by sale. It focuses particularly on vehicles, and on technical and general stores.

Vehicle drawdown

3.2 The Department have two broad categories of vehicle — armoured and non-armoured. Figure 2 shows how armoured vehicles are drawn down. Because the number of armoured vehicles was comparatively small, future requirements for Germany had already been identified and the equipment manager had a placement plan for individual vehicles through to the end of Drawdown, the Department were able to return surplus armoured vehicles directly to the United Kingdom storage depot at Ludgershall. Most of those vehicles which are surplus to the Army's requirements are then sent for disposal by sale.

Figure 2: Movement of Armoured Vehicles

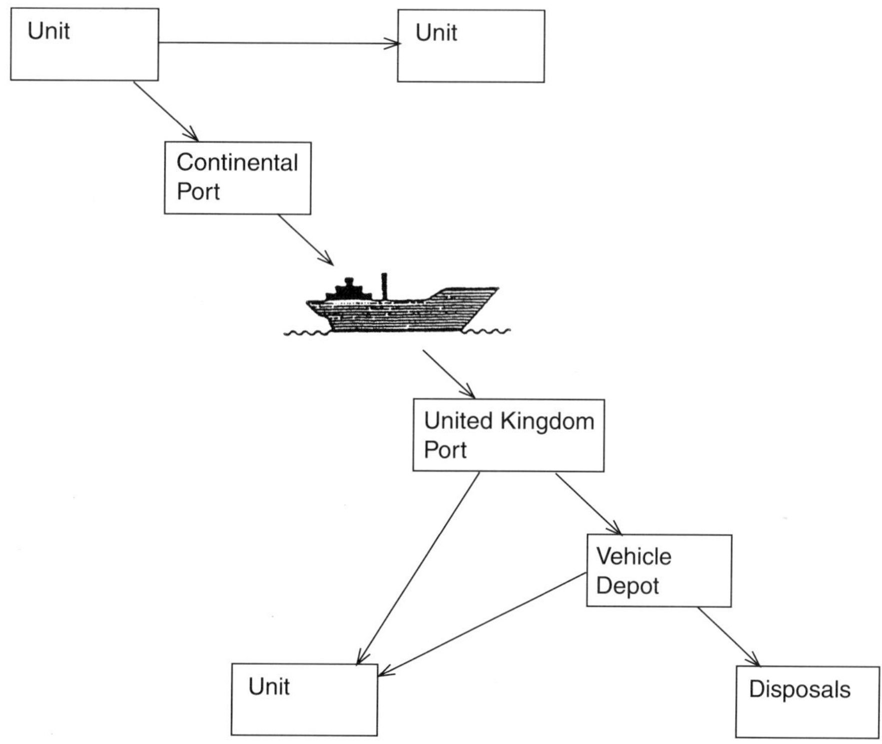

Source: National Audit Office schematic diagram.

Figure 2 shows the routes and options for drawing down armoured vehicles.

3.3 Figure 3 shows how non-armoured vehicles are drawn down. Because of the much larger numbers involved, final decisions have still to be taken on the future requirements for many non-armoured vehicles. Given the scale of the processing task, the Department established the Vehicle Squadron of the Theatre Drawdown Unit in Moenchengladbach. The designated sponsor for each Arm and Service of the Army in Germany, acting on global Army requirements determined by the Department, decide whether vehicles drawn down into the Theatre Drawdown Unit are returned to the United Kingdom vehicle depot, redeployed within Germany, or sent for disposal.

3.4 Many vehicles are sent direct to Disposals in Germany on the instructions of the Department's equipment manager. Others are transferred directly between units in Germany or the United Kingdom on the instructions of the designated sponsor in Germany. The Department considered that this would ease the transition to the new deployments. However, the National Audit Office noted that the Army fleet manager in Germany was having to screen all non-armoured vehicles returned to the Theatre Drawdown Unit in order to identify those superior to others being redeployed elsewhere within Germany by sponsors. Such vehicles then had to be despatched from the Theatre Drawdown Unit to replace inferior vehicles, which in turn had to be sent to the Theatre Drawdown Unit.

Figure 3: Movement of Non-Armoured Vehicles

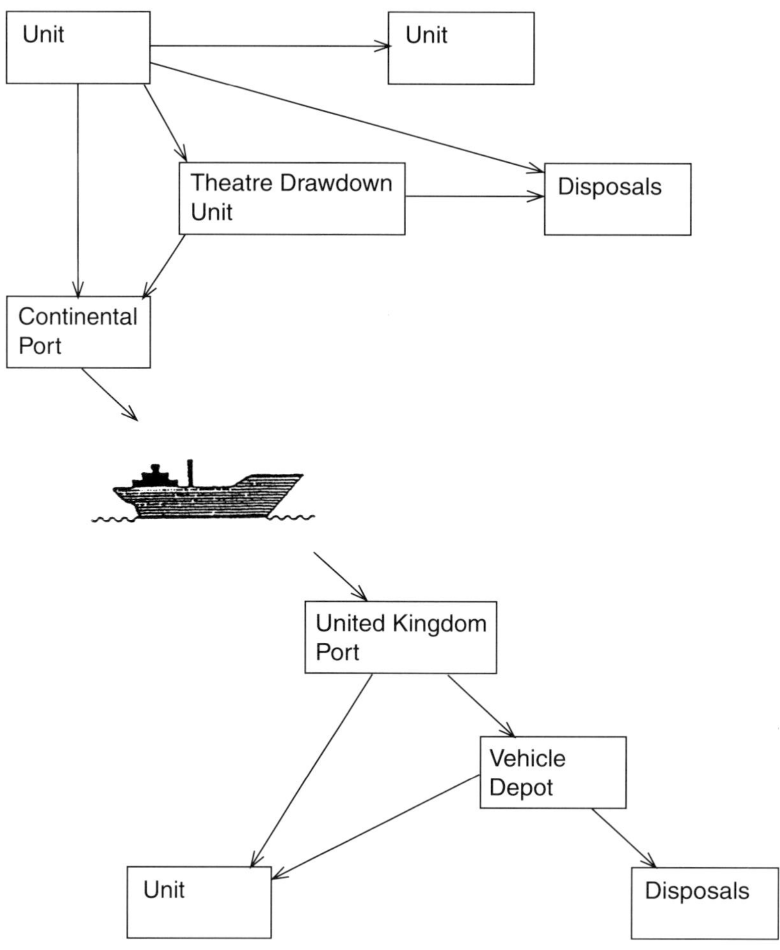

Source: National Audit Office schematic diagram.

This figure shows the routes and options for drawing down non-armoured vehicles.

3.5 The Department were unable to say how often this occurred. But if the vehicle fleet manager had been responsible for deciding what action should be taken on vehicles before they were returned to the Theatre Drawdown Unit, it could have saved transportation and administration costs, and possibly speeded up the return of vehicles to the central inventory. The Department have now actioned a change in policy for Phase 3 of the Drawdown under which vehicle equipment managers will lead on vehicle drawdown.

3.6 Since the beginning of Drawdown the Theatre Drawdown Unit have processed some 3,300 vehicles. In December 1992 they held about 1,600 vehicles of which some had previously been Reserve Stock transferred from depots closed under the Early Closures Programme. About 300 of the vehicles were earmarked as a continuing reserve. The original purchase price of the holdings was some £74 million although many of the older vehicles had little residual value. By the end of Phase 1, in March 1993, the number held had increased to 1,800, of which 1,100 were unserviceable. Most were stored in the open. About 35 per cent of the vehicles, some of which were from the old Reserve Stock, had been on the site for over 12 months and 23 had been in storage for seven years. A small number, around 30, were being held pending call forward for contract repair. In February 1994 the Department informed the National Audit Office that they had reduced the number of vehicles held at the Theatre Drawdown Unit to around 716 (Figure 4).

3.7 In addition to risking deterioration, delays in moving vehicles through the Theatre Drawdown Unit mean that either they were not available for disposal by sale, or they were not being returned to usable stock in the United Kingdom.

3.8 Several factors have contributed to the high number, and often poor condition, of vehicles in the Theatre Drawdown Unit. Some were ex Operation Granby, the majority of which needed repair. However, since most were relatively new, disposal could not be considered without detailed inspection. Similarly, vehicles drawndown could not be classified until inspected. As the Department had yet to complete their review of manpower and equipment needs for the post Options for Change Army (paragraph 2.26),

---

Figure 4: Vehicle Holdings at the Theatre Drawdown Unit

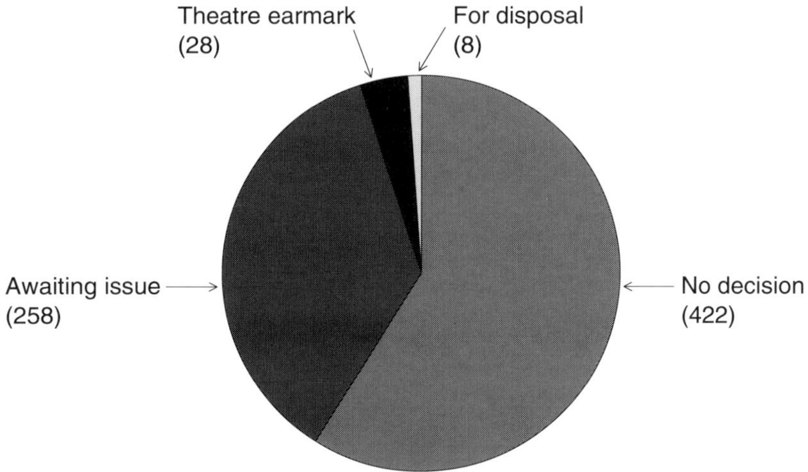

Source: Ministry of Defence.

Figure 4 shows the status of vehicle holdings at the Theatre Drawdown Unit.

they were unable to determine their long term global requirements for vehicles. The effect had been to delay decisions on whether to keep vehicles in Germany, return them to the United Kingdom or sell them. Other factors are:

- vehicles returned to the United Kingdom are driven individually from the Theatre Drawdown Unit to the port of Antwerp by Service personnel. Military drivers, however, are not always available to coincide with the required date for delivery to the port and following the closure of the secure storage facilities at Antwerp under Early Closures, there is no opportunity to hold stocks in reserve for shipping. The National Audit Office suggested to the Department that contract drivers might be a cost effective solution to enable the backlog of vehicles in the Theatre Drawdown Unit to be cleared, and to help maximise use of ship capacity (paragraph 4.6). The Department considered this, but concluded that their use for this task would be uneconomic.

- because the only two vehicle maintenence and storage depots in Germany were disbanded as part of the Early Closures Programme, the Theatre Drawdown Unit has a wide range of vehicle depot tasks for which it is not resourced. Until recently, this prevented the Unit from focusing on its Drawdown responsibilities for which it was originally established. Moreover, because of resource constraints, only limited inspection and repair has been undertaken at the Unit and virtually no maintenance.

Given that the Theatre Drawdown Unit has a wider role from that originally intended, together with the volume of material still to pass through it, the Department now believe it may not be possible to close the facility on completion of Drawdown as initially planned.

3.9 With large numbers of vehicles being returned to the United Kingdom following the Gulf conflict, and because of Drawdown from Germany, the availability of secure storage facilities for non-armoured, and armoured, vehicles has been a problem for the Department. To ease the overcrowding at existing vehicle depots and to ensure that the availability of storage space does not become a constraint on drawdown, Royal Air Force Kemble was made available in mid-1992 as an overspill vehicle storage site. In April 1993 there were some 1,200 vehicles stored there. Kemble was scheduled for-closure and disposal in 1994 but the Department now intend to retain it as an overspill vehicle park until the end of March 1995.

3.10 There is evidence of some delay in returning to usable stock those vehicles sent back to the United Kingdom from Germany. In April 1993 the Department undertook a survey for the National Audit Office of non-armoured vehicles returned from Germany during Early Closures and Phase 1 of Drawdown — some 2,500 of the 8,000 non-armoured vehicles drawn down by the end of Phase 1 were returned to the United Kingdom. Of the 250 vehicles reviewed, 80 were serviceable and had been returned to stock or re-issued. Of the remainder, 42 had been provisionally condemned or sent for disposal, 123 were awaiting repair and 5 remained unclassified. The Department explained that at that time the final numerical requirements for vehicles had not been settled and therefore vehicles were only examined and repaired when there was a specific need for them. The number of vehicles required by the Army has now been largely determined and the Department do not expect a significant backlog awaiting return to usable stock in Phases 2 and 3 of Drawdown.

Main Points:

3.11 **The Department have already drawn down the majority of their armoured vehicles and are continuing their efforts to achieve timely and efficient breakdown of non-armoured vehicles. However, they have recognised:**

- **the scope for more streamlined arrangements so that vehicles returned to the Theatre Drawdown Unit do not have to be sent back out to other units, and different vehicles come back in their place. A change of policy for Phase 3 of Drawdown will eliminate this problem;**

- **the need to maintain their efforts to clear the backlog of vehicles in the Theatre Drawdown Unit; and**

- the need to ensure, particularly in view of the further large quantities yet to be returned, that vehicles sent for storage in the United Kingdom are returned to usable stock or disposed of as quickly as possible. Preferably though, vehicles should not be returned to the United Kingdom for disposal (see paragraph 3.25).

Drawdown of technical and general stores

3.12 The Department's arrangements for drawing down equipment and stores surplus to units' requirements are shown in Figure 5. The bulk are sent to the Stores Squadron of the Theatre Drawdown Unit. There they are processed, and then forwarded to the Department's main storage depot at Dulmen in Germany. Specialist equipment is sometimes returned directly from individual units to the appropriate depot in the United

Figure 5: Movement of Motor Transport, Technical and General Stores

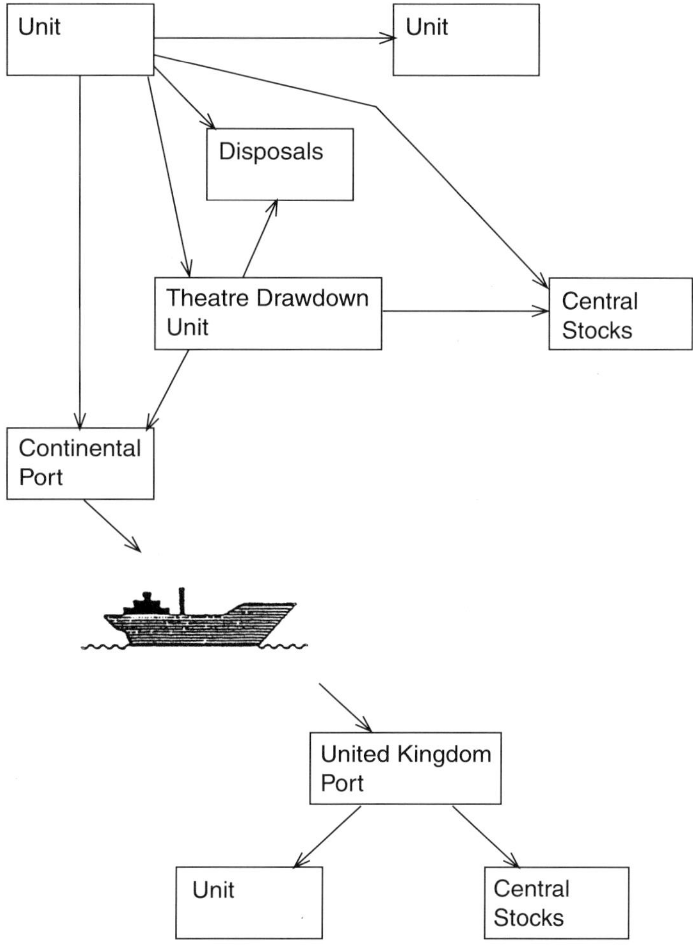

Source: National Audit Office schematic diagram.

This figure shows the routes and options for drawing down equipment and stores.

Kingdom. Items surplus to Army requirements are normally sent for disposal by sale. Overall, the Department expect to drawdown some 1.7 million items, of which nearly 0.7 million were drawn down in Phase 1.

The "shopping list"

3.13 Decisions to return unit stores to the Theatre Drawdown Unit are based on a "shopping list" of items for which the Department have identified a continuing need. In March 1993 the list included some 309,000 items.

3.14 Items not on the shopping list are either disposed of locally, or sent to the Disposals Depot for sale by them. During Phase 1 approximately 20 per cent of the items received by the Theatre Drawdown Unit were subsequently re-directed to the Sales Depot approximately 8 miles away thus incurring additional handling costs. The Department stated that most of these were items of Nuclear, Biological and Chemical Clothing which had passed their shelf life and which had to be made unserviceable by the Theatre Drawdown Unit before transfer to the Disposals Depot. However, other items were re-directed because changes to the shopping list of items to be disposed of had not been made known to units in the process of drawing down. The Department are now updating the list more regularly to reduce unnecessary processing of returned items.

3.15 In placing items on the shopping list, the Department have had no regard to the value of the item, and to the processing and transport costs involved in returning an item to the Theatre Drawdown Unit and, from there, to the storage depot at Dulmen. But Figure 6 shows that 12 per cent of unit returns to the Drawdown Unit represented 64 per cent of the value. The average value of some 76 per cent of the returns was £7. The Department estimate that some £2.5 million worth of stores have been recovered in this way which the Department consider worthwhile, particularly where the stores concerned were already in short supply.

3.16 The National Audit Office recognise that in assessing the viability of returning low value items to the Theatre Drawdown Unit, the Department need to weigh the following factors against the cost of processing and storing: the cost and availability of

replacements; the quantities being processed together; possible sale value and whether the alternative would be to pay for disposal. In the light of the National Audit Office's observations, the Department have amended the shopping list criteria to include replacement costs. This should lead to better informed decisions.

Liaison with United Kingdom supply depots

3.17 The depots continue to issue stores in response to demands from units in the process of drawing down until they receive a unit disbandment or movement notice. Units are responsible for issuing these notices, and for cancelling outstanding demands that are no longer needed.

3.18 In early 1993, the Department realised that 26 of the 100 units which had already drawn down or moved had failed to comply with these procedures. Consequently, issues of stores were still being made to their previous addresses. In one case, despite requesting that their outstanding demands be cancelled, a unit continued to receive unwanted stock against more than 500 item headings — or 5 per cent of their total inventory. The Department have now taken steps to ensure that units drawing down notify the inventory control point in the United Kingdom of their closure or movement plans.

3.19 As regards items returned from Germany during the Early Closure Programme, much was sent directly to depots in the United Kingdom before the Stores Company of the Theatre Drawdown Unit was established. However, the volume of equipment and stores returned from the Gulf conflict at around the same time overwhelmed the United Kingdom storage depots. Processing of this equipment was given priority over that returned from Germany, with the result that some 120 containers from the Early Closures Programme and Phase 1 of Drawdown were awaiting attention at Donnington for 12 months or more. As the Department were unaware of the contents of the containers, they were unable to take account of what had been returned in establishing their reprovisioning requirements. They expect, however, that the introduction throughout 1994 of new computer systems will enable inventory managers to control the movement and location of stores. This should ensure that the problem does not arise again.

Figure 6: Theatre Drawdown Unit — Stores Company

Percentage of Issues to Central Stocks by Store Category

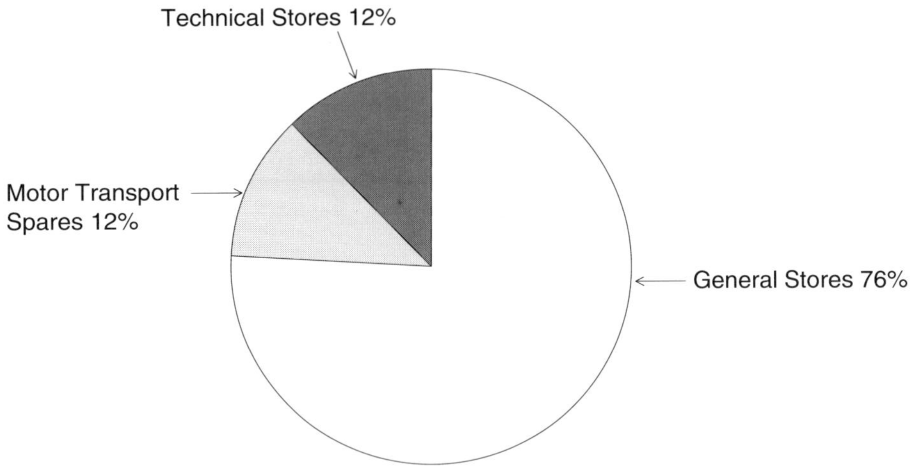

Value of Issues to Central Stocks by Stores Category

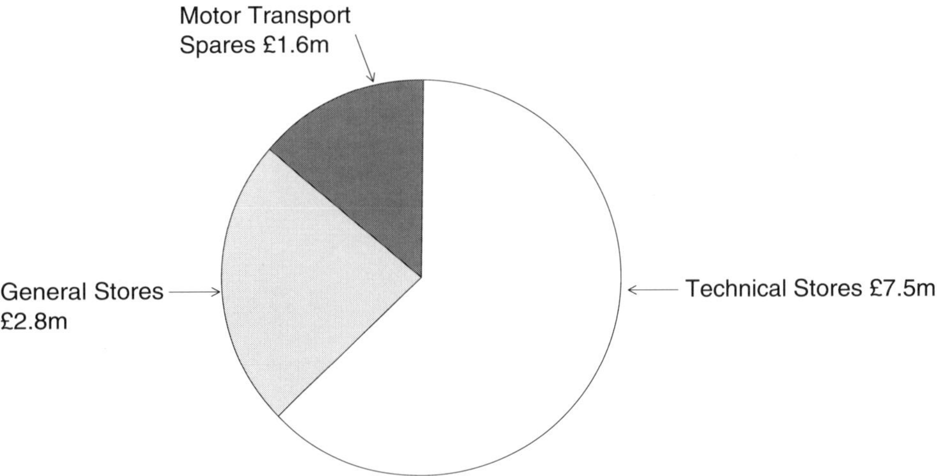

Note: The period to which these issues relate is April 1992 to March 1993.
Source: Ministry of Defence.

Figure 6 shows the percentage and value of issues to Central Stocks.

3.20 The Department have now reduced the backlog at Donnington to a more manageable processing time of four to six weeks, and during Phases 2 and 3 of Drawdown most returning stock will go via the Theatre Drawdown Unit to Dulmen. In view of processing delays at Donnington during Phase 1 of drawdown, a large proportion of the £90 million holdings of spares, including engines and major assemblies, from 23 Base Workshop in Germany, were sent to the stores depot at Dulmen. This workshop is the largest unit being disbanded under the Drawdown Programme.

3.21　Initially, this resulted in a processing backlog at Dulmen but this has since been cleared. It has also had the effect of placing in Dulmen specialist equipment, amounting to some 30 per cent of total holdings, used solely for base repair activities which will, in future, be carried out only in the United Kingdom. The Department are in the process of determining whether there remains a requirement for this equipment and if so, where it should be located. Only those items deemed essential will be returned to the United Kingdom, with those not required being sent for disposal, probably in Germany where they are expected to command a higher price.

Main Points:

3.22　**In drawing down technical and general stores, the Department should:**

- **ensure that items ultimately destined for disposal are not first sent to the Theatre Drawdown Unit. This incurs additional handling costs;**

- **have closer regard to the costs and benefits of returning low value items to the central inventory. The recent attribution of replacement costs to items on the "shopping list" may lead to better informed judgements in this area;**

- **in view of the potential provisioning advantages of having returned equipment and stores recorded on the central inventory, avoid recurrence of significant delays in processing returned items. This will be a particular challenge as further large quantities of items are drawn down in Phases 2 and 3;**

- **ensure that items of equipment sent to Units already closed are fully accounted for; and**

- **continue their review of equipment holdings at Dulmen to determine what should be retained there and what should be returned to the United Kingdom. The results of this review will help inform the wider survey on the future retention of Dulmen.**

Disposals by sale

3.23　Drawdown has presented the Department with the need to dispose of vast quantities of items surplus to their requirements and, in so doing, the opportunity to generate income. Partly in recognition of the task ahead of them, in August 1991 the Department transferred responsibility for the sales depot in Moenchengladbach to their centralised Sales Directorate in the United Kingdom, although sales continued to be handled locally in Germany.

3.24　In 1992–93 receipts from all disposals by sale in Germany (not just those relating to Army surpluses) amounted to £5.18 million. The Department estimate that they will generate further receipts of £8.5 million by the end of Phase 3 in March 1995 (Figure 7). However, future sales and prices in Germany will be influenced by the sales activities of the United States and German Forces who are both disposing of their surplus equipment and stores in the same market place.

Figure 7: Disposal Sales Depot, Germany — Value of receipts for each phase of Drawdown

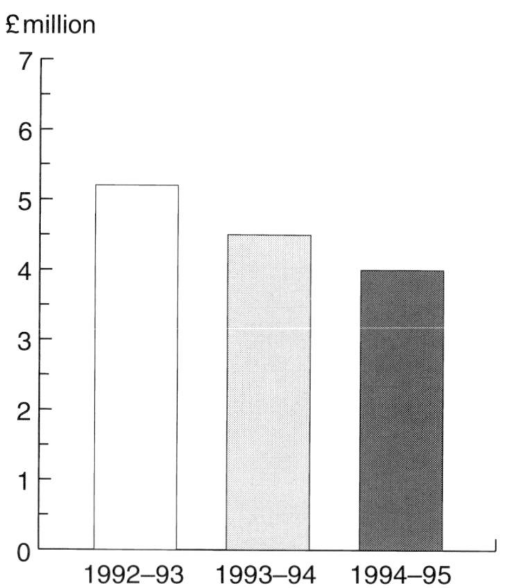

Source: Ministry of Defence statistics.
Note: The values for 1993-94 and 1994-95 are the Department's estimates.

Figure 7 shows disposal sales receipts for Phase 1 and estimates for Phases 2 and 3.

3.25 In 1992–93 some 76 per cent (£4.0 million) of the Department's sales in Germany related to vehicles. The Department have been unable to reach agreement with the German Government to allow the sale of armoured vehicles in Germany. Accordingly they must be returned to the United Kingdom to be sold. Non-armoured vehicles may, however, be sold in Germany and, in the main, they are — some 3,800 vehicles, including trailers, were sent to the Disposal Depot in 1992–93 alone. This not only avoided the cost of transportation and handling involved in returning vehicles to the United Kingdom, but the Department state that the sale price of vehicles is usually somewhat higher in Germany than in the United Kingdom. The National Audit Office noted, however, that:

- the Department's sample survey of vehicles returned to the United Kingdom by the end of Phase 1 of Drawdown showed that roughly 16 per cent had been condemned or sent for disposal by sale (paragraph 3.10). If this sample were representative of the 2,500 non-armoured vehicles returned to the United Kingdom by the end of Phase 1, then in excess of 400 of these vehicles will have been sent for disposal in the United Kingdom. The Department consider that now future requirements are clearer, the numbers likely to be sent for disposal will be much reduced. They also informed the National Audit Office that they are now taking steps to ensure closer co-ordination between Germany and the United Kingdom regarding vehicles repatriated;

- the Department's local Sales Depot staff in Germany estimate that the sale price of some vehicles can be enhanced by around 20 per cent if they are in running condition. Vehicles sold as non-runners often have only minor defects, such as a flat battery. In September 1993 the Department recruited a civilian fitter for the purpose of making the necessary repairs. Of the 3,200 engined vehicles sent for disposal in 1992–93, some 800 (25 per cent) were classified as runners;

- in February 1993, Internal Audit criticised the practice of cannibalising potential sales vehicles, often for relatively low value items which, nevertheless, rendered the vehicle a non-runner. They estimated that runners could command

up to £400 (at July 93 rates of exchange) more than non-runners, depending on the type of vehicle.

3.26 Now that surplus vehicles are arising as a result of unit closures and amalgamations, the Department agree with the National Audit Office that it would be beneficial for Equipment Managers from all three Services to consult prior to disposal action being taken. To that end the Department are introducing a mechanism to enable such tri-Service liaison to take place.

Main Points:

3.27 **The Department have already achieved sales receipts in excess of £5 million. As they seek to achieve maximum benefit from the large quantities of surplus equipment and stores likely to arise from the remaining phases of Drawdown, the Department should:**

- **do more to ensure that where possible vehicles are sold in Germany rather than transported to the United Kingdom. The fact that some vehicles returned to the United Kingdom have then been sold suggests that there is a need for closer co-ordination of requirements between Germany and the United Kingdom;**

- **give closer attention to ensuring that sales vehicles are cannibalised only when it is essential and cost effective to do so;**

- **enhance the sales value of vehicles by, where cost effective, making minor repairs to turn them into "runners". The Department have recently recruited a fitter for this process; and**

- **consolidate arrangements for offering surplus vehicles to the other Services before disposing of them.**

Part 4: The movement and control of equipment and stores

4.1 This part examines the Department's arrangements for moving equipment and stores between Germany and the United Kingdom, and their accounting for equipment and stores during drawdown.

The movement of equipment and stores

Audit Criterion

Whether the Department evaluate the relative cost effectiveness of using military or civilian transport.

4.2 The Department's policy is to use where possible military vehicles and drivers in preference to commercial organisations to undertake the rundown of the British Army of the Rhine. But the nature or size of the task often means that commercial transport is used. For example, for the large number of containers required for unit moves and when National Bridge Classification Regulations prohibit use of military vehicles. Some use is also made of commercial rail freight for special requirements like ammunition, or to meet a shortfall in military transport.

4.3 The marginal costs of using Service transport and drivers are significantly less than the full cost of the commercial option. For example, in terms of carrying capacity the use of one rail wagon would equate to about two military vehicles; but the cost of using that one wagon would be ten times the military option. However, if Service transport were fully costed, the balance would swing in the other direction. The choice depends, therefore, on the value to the Department of work which military personnel and vehicles would otherwise be used for.

Audit Criterion

Whether contracts with commercial carriers are let competitively and clearly specify Department's requirements.

4.4 The Department have let some 250 contracts centrally in Germany, all for under £10,000, which have been for Drawdown related movements by road and sea. National Audit Office examination of a small sample (5 per cent) showed that the specifications were clear; that there had been competing tenders in each case; and that the Department had accepted the contractor offering the lowest price. It appeared to the National Audit Office, however, that there might be scope for the Department to reduce their administrative effort and achieve better prices by combining requirements into fewer contracts and/or exploring the scope for running contracts which they could call on as and when required. But the Department said that in view of the complexity of the task it was impracticable to aggregate requirements, because the movements were between 38 locations in Germany and 48 in the United Kingdom, using a mix of vehicles and containers and a complex matrix of routes.

4.5 In October 1992 the Department diverted for use during Operation Grapple one of the Royal Fleet Auxiliary Landing Ship Logistics, used primarily to re-supply Germany, but also used in the Drawdown programme on the return leg to the United Kingdom. They replaced it with a commercial roll-on roll-off vessel, the NORNEWS SERVICE on a time-charter basis. A tender list of ten ships was submitted to the Department's Shipping Committee in the United Kingdom by the Government Freight Agent and the Government Freight Marketing Representative. The Department told the National Audit Office that five vessels met the specification and that the NORNEWS SERVICE was the cheapest. There was not a full record, however, of the tender analysis in that the comparative capability of the ten ships was not recorded.

Audit Criterion

Whether the Department utilise the capacity of the available transport.

Figure 8: Utilisation of Chartered Ship — Nornews Service

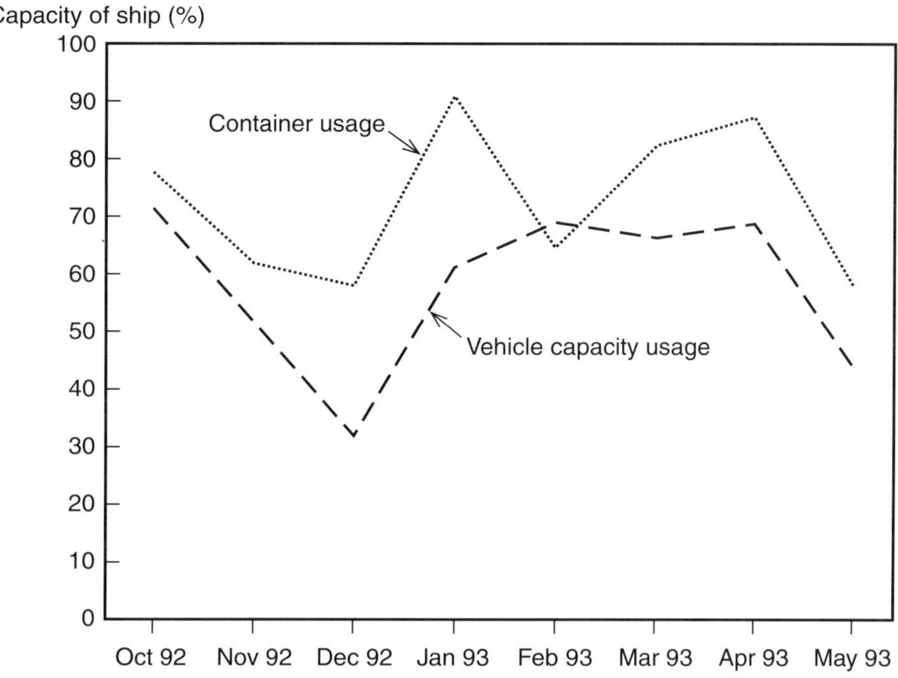

Source: Ministry of Defence statistics.
Note: Container usage and vehicle capacity usage rates are actual utilisation rates based on the Department's statistical returns but take no account of the Department's statement that as the width of some military vehicles reduced available capacity, utilisation was actually higher.

Figure 8 shows the utilisation statistics for NORNEWS Ferry.

4.6 The NORNEWS SERVICE cost the Department £4,000 a day; they paid the same amount, irrespective of the capacity used, and by July 1993 they had spent some £1.04 million. National Audit Office analysis (Figure 8) of the Department's utilisation of the NORNEWS SERVICE showed that over a seven month period the ship's container capacity was on average some 74 per cent utilised, and that on average 57 per cent of the vehicle capacity was used. The Department stated however that utilisation was higher because the width of certain vehicles precluded the maximum use of all the ship's capacity on most of the sailings. They also informed the National Audit Office that they had chartered a vessel with a greater capacity than the in-service Landing Ship Logistic because at the time it was required, it was the cheapest available which met the requirement for on and off-loading of heavy armoured vehicles whilst also providing an acceptable overall capacity. In the event the Department were able to return more stores and equipment than would have been possible using a Landing Ship Logistic alone. The Department told the National Audit Office that to achieve the same level of movements it would have been necessary to charter additional ferry capacity at a cost of around £400,000.

4.7 Nevertheless, the utilisation figures suggest that the Department had the shipping capacity to repatriate more equipment and stores than they did during Phase 1. This might have helped to reduce holdings at the Theatre Drawdown Unit.

Main Points:

4.8 **The Department use military drivers and transport in preference to commercial carriers. However, where commercial carriers are used, their contracting arrangements have been for the most part satisfactory. However:**

- **the basis for the Department's choice of a chartered vessel for the resupply of British Forces in Germany and Drawdown tasks was not fully documented in that the comparative capability of the ten ships was not recorded; and**

- **the commercial chartered vessel was not used to its full capacity on its trips from Germany to the United Kingdom, although it moved more equipment than would have been possible with the Service vessel.**

Accounting for equipment and stores

4.9 As a result of drawdown, enormous and exceptional quantities of equipment and stores are being moved within Germany, and between Germany and the United Kingdom. The National Audit Office therefore examined whether the Department had maintained normal accounting standards and safeguards.

Audit Criteria

Whether there are controls to minimise the risk of fraud and losses.

Whether the Department are able to account for equipment and stores throughout unit moves and closures.

4.10 The Department require that units in the process of drawing down maintain normal accounting procedures and control. And partly to ensure that this is done, the Department's internal auditors have carried out 20 pre-closure audits at units to ensure that proper controls were in place, and also four post-closure audits. In general, Internal Audit have found that accounting standards have been maintained at units in the process of drawing down. However, both Internal Audit and the National Audit Office noted significant problems with the clearance of accounts for units that had already closed.

4.11 When equipment and stores are sent from one establishment to another, the sender raises an issue voucher. The sender's account is not clear, however, until they have documented evidence—the receipt voucher—that the goods have been received. As units continue to issue and receive equipment and stores during their drawdown period, stores accounts are often uncleared when the units finally close. Consequently custodial units, either in the United Kingdom or in Germany, are nominated to administer the accounts of closed units until those accounts are cleared. Custodial units do not receive extra resources to carry out this work, which in the case of some of the large units closing, can be considerable. For example, a major unit, 23 Base Workshop is likely to hand over 20–30 four-drawer filing cabinets of accounts paperwork to its custodial units.

4.12 The National Audit Office visited the custodial units of two units which had closed under the Early Closures Programme, one which had closed early in Phase 1 of Drawdown, and six units which were in the course of drawing down. These showed that clearance of outstanding accounts was a problem. Whilst not necessarily representative of all units involved in Drawdown, these findings were consistent with those of Internal Audit during their pre- and post-closure audits. By February 1994 two of the accounts of the seven units closed under the Early Closure Programme (completed in March 1992), and two of the 109 units closed or moved during Phase 1 of Drawdown (completed in March 1993), had been cleared.

4.13 From their examination in March 1993 of the accounts of two of the units disbanded during Early Closures, the National Audit Office noted that:

- in one case, a very large equipment and stores holding organisation, there had been a virtual loss of control during disbandment of the accounts. Records and supporting vouchers were incomplete, and important demand registers were missing. Uncleared vouchers at the custodial unit included some relating to vehicles, sub-machine guns, rifles and other automatic weapons. The Department were immediately notified. They told the National Audit Office that subsequent internal investigation had shown that no physical loss of weapons had occurred and that all had been accounted for.

- by February 1994 no further action had been taken to reconcile the considerable number of other vouchers still outstanding although the Department had addressed the measures necessary for formal closure of the accounts. Included in the small sample examined by the National Audit Office were several relating to vehicles and one, which had been outstanding for nearly three years, for 60lbs of plastic explosive and 110 detonators. The Department were notified in mid February 1994 and responded quickly and positively to the National Audit Office. The Department's initial investigations suggested that all of the items had been expended during training and, therefore, that the problem was an accounting irregularity only. The Department advised that it was taking steps to confirm that no loss had occurred. They added that all vehicles had been accounted for. The Department have now issued instructions reminding Commanders at all levels of the need for correct accounting procedures, and prompt action to resolve any discrepancies. The programme of work for Internal Audit in Germany has been amended to include examination of ammunition accounting procedures across the Command.

- as regards the other unit account examined, the custodial unit had been holding some 14,500 returned receipt vouchers (acknowledging receipt of items by other units) for up to 12 months, but had not processed them to clear the account. Again, the National Audit Office immediately raised this with the Department, who responded quickly. The Department told the National Audit Office that by February 1994 they had, as a result of considerable effort, reduced the number of outstanding vouchers to 214, and that in doing this they had identified 114 discrepancies on items with an overall book value of about £97,000.

4.14 Delays in processing the vast quantities of items returned to the United Kingdom have almost certainly been a major factor in the Department's inability to clear unit accounts. However, Internal Audit identified instances where receipt vouchers returned from the United Kingdom had been addressed to the unit that had closed, rather than to the custodial unit. This difficulty should reduce since units returning items to the Theatre Drawdown Unit are given receipts at the time of delivery; this will greatly simplify the tasks of closing unit accounts.

4.15 Further difficulties in clearing accounts may arise when custodial units themselves close, and custodial responsibility is passed to other units. Given the number of units drawing down in Phases 2 and 3, this situation could arise. For example in March 1993, 23 Base Workshop had not started work on clearing the account of 37 Rhine Workshop, for which it is the custodial unit. A considerable effort will be required, at a time when the Workshop is pre-occupied with its own drawdown arrangements, to clear the large and growing number of outstanding vouchers they hold. If this task is not achieved before they disband, they will have to hand over their own accounts, and the accounts for which they curently have custodial responsibilities, to another custodial unit.

National Audit Office test checks

4.16 In the light of the Department's difficulties in clearing unit accounts, the National Audit Office undertook limited test checks to see whether items could actually be traced.

4.17 A total of 80 vouchers relating to items issued by units in Germany which had closed or were closing down were selected to see whether the items had reached their intended destinations — depots in the United Kingdom, and the Theatre Drawdown Unit in Germany. In all but eight cases the National Audit Office were able to confirm that the items had been received. Although the untraced items were mostly low value, they also included twelve firearms and three weapon accessories. The Department were advised of these discrepancies. Following a further investigation, they advised that the weapons and accessories had all been traced.

4.18 During their visit to the United Kingdom depot at Donnington, the National Audit Office were told that some 600 discrepancy reports relating to equipment accounts of units which disbanded under Early Closures and Phase 1 of Drawdown were being actioned. The Department expect many of these discrepancies to be resolved but in some instances write-off action will be required.

23 Base Workshop, Germany

4.19 Because of its size and the value of its equipment and stores holdings, the National Audit Office visited 23 Base Workshop to see how the unit was implementing its drawdown plan. The Workshop is due to close on 31 March 1994. The National Audit Office noted two key areas of concern relating to accounting and control:

- the Department were having difficulty with the electronic accounting systems at the Workshop. They were concerned that because of errors in the electronically controlled stores account, which is valued at some £45 million, there will be large numbers of discrepancies to be reconciled when the unit closes;

- the Department discontinued rolling stocktake at the Workshop in June 1992, but resumed activity in February 1993. The Department accept that rolling stocktakes should not have been discontinued without prior approval of the appropriate stores accounting authority;

- the Workshop has an equipment account with over 9,000 item headings — many held in large quantities, and estimated by the Department to be worth some £65 million. In preparation for closure, the Department had checked 89 per cent of items in the account by March 1993, but had found only 68 per cent. Of the 3,500 line items unreconciled, they had found some 2,995 by February 1994. They expect other equipment to reappear as individual areas of the Workshop close.

Main Points:

4.20 **Maintaining normal standards of accounting and control during a period of exceptional movement and upheaval is not easy. However, the Department have recognised the importance of applying their usual procedures, and on the whole, units drawing down have achieved this. Nevertheless, the National Audit Office identified a number of areas which give cause for concern and require continuing management attention:**

- **clearing the accounts of units which, in some cases, have been closed for at least 23 months;**

- **transactions relating to weapons;**

- **ensuring that vouchers acknowledging receipt of items are not returned to closed units, but to their custodial units;**

- **being alive to the particular difficulties which may arise as accounting responsibility is passed from one custodial unit to another. Given the difficulties which custodial units have already faced, it seems to the National Audit Office that there is a risk of a serious breakdown in control unless responsibilities, and changes to them, are closely charted and controlled;**

- **resolving the accounting problems and equipment discrepancies at 23 Base Workshop before the unit account is passed on to custodial units;**

- **ensuring that units maintain normal stocktaking throughout their drawdown period, unless prior authorisation is given by the appropriate stores accounting officer; and**

- **ensuring that the discrepancies which have come to light are properly investigated.**

Reports by the Comptroller and Auditor General
Session 1993–94

The Comptroller and Auditor General has to date, in Session 1993–94, presented to the House of Commons the following reports under Section 9 of the National Audit Act, 1983:

Printed in the United Kingdom for HMSO
Dd 5061989   4/94   C9   3398B   4235   280230   Job No. 941305